# WATER BABIES

## *How to Teach Your Baby to Swim*

By
**Gina Ambrose**
**and**
**Gretchen Mack**

Printed in the United States of America
First Printing, 1998

Library of Congress-in-Publication Data
        Ambrose, Gina, and
        Mack, Gretchen
        "Water Babies," How To Teach Your Baby To Swim

For Information or to order call
888-743-4887

Cover photograph -- Shanti Okawa, 10 months old, September 1996.

# TABLE OF CONTENTS

# PART ONE

**Gina and one of her first water babies**

# DEDICATION FROM GRETCHEN

I would like to dedicate this book and extend a very special thank you to:

Crystal Scarborough — who taught me to teach children to swim.

Gina, my precious daughter and very first water baby, whose love of water and love for the babies she teaches have made it possible to write this book!

The thousands of children who have gone through the "Water Babies" program and come out with a love for swimming.

And the parents who through this book will make their babies happy swimmers.

# DEDICATION FROM GINA

I would like to dedicate this book and extend a very special thank you to:

My first teacher ... my mother, Gretchen Mack, with all my love.

Connie Mallory ... a heartfelt thank you for all the care and love you have given throughout the years, managing Water Babies Swim School.

And all my Water Babies who throughout the past 30 years have made my life joyous.

# HISTORY AND INTRODUCTION
## BY GRETCHEN MACK

*This is a personal welcome to you and your baby ...
and a special invitation to join me in one of the loves of my life,
"Water Babies!"*

This is a practical book designed to help you teach your own child to swim the "Water Babies" way. The concept of "Water Babies" was born not long after the birth of my daughter, Gina. She was the first baby I taught to swim. By the time she was fifteen months old, she was jumping happily off the side of the pool and coming up for a breath. The Oakland Tribune newspaper featured her in an article and I had people calling me from ten different cities asking me to teach their child to swim.

As a single alone, I started Peter Pan Playschool to be able to support my children and have them with me. The swim school began one day when I decided to clean out the old pool in the back yard and teach my children to swim. I had been a competitive diver when I was younger, so swimming had always been a big part of my life. I wanted to give those children the joy of being in the water as well as assure myself that they would be safe around the pool.

I visited Crystal Scarborough, a baby swimming teacher, who had become famous for her work with the movie stars' children. After working with Crystal, I came back and starting teaching the little ones at the preschool. I also brought back some flipper fins which Crystal had designed to help the children swim more efficiently. These fins became a wonderful teaching tool and have made a tremendous difference in the time that it takes for a child to be independent in the water. We still use flipper fins and have them available if you are unable to find them in your area.

This book contains information on our history, pictures of some of our babies, and most important, instructions on how to teach your child to become a "Water Baby." Gina has a very successful swim school in Campbell, California. It is filled with swimming babies from the time the doors open in the morning until they close at night. She runs the school with the help of her invaluable manager, Connie, and ten other teachers, one of whom is my grandson, John. We realize that there are many places where there are no such schools, so we have designed this volume to help parents teach their babies to swim.

Welcome, . . . I hope you learn a lot from following the directions. I am certain you and your baby will greatly benefit from our experience, and I know that both of you will come away with a renewed confidence and respect for the water and have fun while you are learning.

# A MESSAGE FROM GINA AMBROSE

I suppose you could say that I was the original Water Baby. For as long as I can remember, I have loved the water, swimming, and especially teaching babies to swim.

I started swimming competitively when I was five years old and swam for the YMCA in Berkeley. At age nine, we moved to the Santa Clara Valley where I was coached by the renowned George Haines. For the next ten years I competed in swim meets all over the country and loved every minute of it. I finally stopped competitive swimming and started teaching babies in our back yard pool. After we had outgrown our pool, Mom found our present site in Campbell, where we've been for the past 29 years. My mother retired to South Carolina. I own Water Babies Swim School now, and we have classes going on most of the year.

The pictures you see throughout the book are some of the Water Babies Swim School students from today and yesterday. There have been so many children over the years that there is no way we could mention the names or show pictures of all of them. Each and every child, however, has a special place in our hearts and memories; they will always be our "water babies."

Imagine an Olympic size pool with babies, from two months old to five or six years old . . . and that might give you some idea of the number of babies that have been taught to swim at Water Babies Swim School. We dedicate this book to all of you, past, present and future!

# PART TWO

**Can you believe I'm really swimming under water?**

# TEACHING YOUR BABY TO SWIM

## LESSONS FOR INFANTS

The steps in teaching an infant to swim are the same whether you are a teacher with several students or a parent with one child. The first lesson varies according to any prior experience that the child might have had in the water. If the child is less than six months old, she has probably had little experience in water other than the bath tub. Some have been in a backyard pool, but few have had lessons at this age. Therefore we are going to assume for our purposes that the child in question has had little exposure to the water. We will start from scratch.

**Welcome to water babies**

## GETTING BABY ACCUSTOMED TO THE WATER

First, you must introduce the baby to the water. The tiny babies take to the water very easily and are usually not afraid. Our goal in this first lesson is to simply get the child acclimated to the new surroundings and to the instructor, whether it is Mom, Dad, or someone else.

Have fun with your baby. Hold her close as you enter the water. Smile and let her know this is a "fun time" and that there is nothing to be afraid of.

**Our first lesson**

# STEP ONE: "KICKING"

Most babies less than six months will kick automatically. They have a natural inclination or reflex to kick, but some lose this at after about six months of age. Every child is different, however, so don't compare your baby. Never feel as if you are in competition with your neighbor as each child needs to learn at his own pace. It doesn't matter if the baby is slow or fast, he is going to end up being a wonderful swimmer with a little bit of practice.

**This is one time that it's all right to kick**

# LEARNING TO "KICK"

1. Put the child on your shoulder as if he were giving you a big hug.

2. Place one hand on each of his calves and start rotating his legs up and around toward his bottom as if he were riding a little bicycle.

3. Keep his feet under the surface of the water so the baby can feel the resistance.

4. At the same time, walk backwards so the baby will feel he is going forward.

5. Keep the baby moving, so he becomes accustomed to constant motion. That way if he falls in or slips off your shoulder, he will want to swim.

6. When the child starts to kick, hold him at the waist or under the arms, with his bottom up, and continue to walk backward and let him kick.

7. If he only kicks sporadically, place a bright toy or something he likes in front of him. He will usually go forward for the object.

## STEP TWO: "DIPPING" THE BABY

This will be the most important step you take in teaching your baby to swim, so don't rush through it. Try to pick a time when your baby is the happiest and start with the following steps:

# LEARNING TO "DIP"

1. Start by putting one hand on the baby's chest and the other hand over the back and neck. Put one or two fingers up the back of the head for support.

2. You are going to dip the baby "forward." Never dip a baby vertically. This will cause her to get water up her nose and end up with a definite dislike of "dipping."

3. As you count, "One, two, . . . three," giving a little bounce on each count, bring the baby down toward the water.

4. On the fourth count, blow firmly in the baby's face. This will cause her to stop her breath and hold it for an instant.

5. Continue blowing until the baby's face is in the water, making sure this is a quick continuous movement.

6. Just "skim" the baby's face in the water at first. Never take her whole head under the water at the beginning. That is too long a period of time, and the baby could take a breath under water and come up coughing and choking.

7. Guide the head under with the palm of your hand and water won't get up her nose.

8. When you finish the dip give her a big hug and praise her efforts.

9. Practice your dips until you can do two or three in a row with breaths in between.

You'll soon find that you won't have to blow in baby's face any longer. The children quickly come to know what you're going to do when you count to three. They simply hold their breath, go under, and stay until they need another breath. The parent is there to help them come up. The tiny babies will end up turning over and floating on their backs.

By the end of a series of lessons, the baby should be holding his breath for four or five seconds at a time. This may seem like an eternity to a parent, but if a baby falls in the water and is able to hold its breath, you won't think it's too long at all. That is, after all, the whole idea. In every lesson, the time under water should be lengthened an instant.

# STEP THREE: "LETTING GO"

Start with "kicking" and "dipping" as learned in the first two steps. Kick for a minute or so, then practice your dips for a few minutes. Try to lengthen out the time under the water so she will hold her breath for a second or two.

Then move to Step Three, "Letting Go," when the baby is doing well on her tummy and holding her breath.

**Don't you think that I'm incredible?**

# LEARNING TO "LET GO"

1. Put your hands in the "dipping" position.

2. Count to three, blow, "dip," and "release" your hands from the baby's body an inch or two, but only for an instant.

3. Then catch the child again and bring her up. If she is agreeable, repeat this step two or three times.

4. Don't worry. It's not like you're letting her go and hoping she'll come up again sometime before Christmas. You are still very much in control.

5. By the end of the lesson, you will usually be able to release the baby for an instant at a time without apprehension.

# STEP FOUR: "RELEASING"

Now that we've learned to "let go" for a second or two, the time comes to work on "releasing" the baby. If both parents are in the water, you can pass the baby between the two of you. If not, you can easily do this on your own.

In this step, we learn to give the baby a gentle push toward the parent or helper. The parent or helper catches the baby. This adds another second or so under water helping to develop the baby's breath control. The baby should start kicking on his own and "swimming" for a short distance. After a little practice, both of you will be very comfortable with this step.

**Catch me, Mom!**

# LEARNING TO "RELEASE"

1. Count to three slowly.

2. Blow in the baby's face.

3. "Dip" the baby.

4. "Let go" of baby, releasing him and at the same time give him a gentle push toward the parent or helper.

# STEP FIVE: "TURNING OVER AND FLOATING"

This step, turning the babies over on their backs, comes during the third or fourth lesson. Teaching the baby to turn over and float is as much a safety lesson as a lesson in swimming.

**Hi there, Mom!**

# LEARNING TO "TURN OVER AND FLOAT"

1.  Take the baby from a front position, looking at the baby straight on.

2.  Count to three.

3.  Blow in baby's face.

4.  Dip baby as usual and then very quickly lift and turn baby over onto his back in one motion, taking care not to turn him over while still under the water. Make sure his face is out of the water as quickly as possible.

5.  Turn the baby to your left if you are right-handed (or to the right, if you are left-handed) so you have constant control. Your hand should be over the top of the baby with your other hand cupping the child's head. Put your index finger down the baby's back, which gives him more support.

6.  While baby is on his back with your hand under his head, put the other hand on top of the tummy just for support until you get baby in a comfortable position.

7.  Then take your hand from baby's tummy but keep it close in case baby starts to move. The other hand stays supportive under the head.

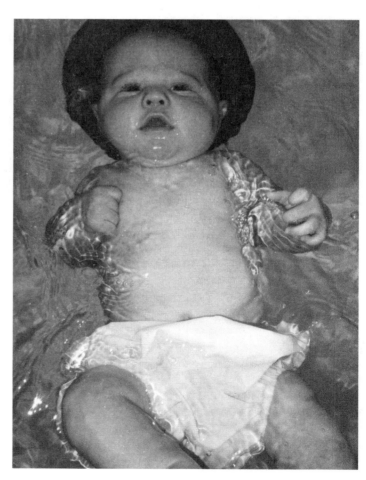

8.  Let the baby float on his back with your hand supporting his head. Let him relax and feel the water around his body. Try not to give him too much support, or he may start to pull his legs down or try to sit up. Let the water do the work for you. Make sure water is not getting into baby's nose or mouth at this point.

## STEP SIX: "PULLING MOTION"

    After the baby gets the idea of "turning over and floating" and she has done it many times, we can be somewhat assured that if she were to fall into the water, she'd have the idea to turn over on her back and get a breath. This may take a bit of time. So be patient. In this next step, we start the "pulling motion."

    Take your hand from baby's head and start pulling under the back of the head and neck, moving the baby at all times. It can be in a stationary position or you can move through the water with the baby.

# LEARNING THE "PULLING MOTION"

1. As you lift the baby up and turn her over on her back, let her relax there for a moment and get used to feeling the water around her body.

2. Put your hands underneath the back of the head and neck supporting her.

3. Start pulling your hands out from under her head one at a time, gently, slowly, and evenly. Do not rock the baby back and forth.

4. Keep your thumbs right along the baby's ears so if she starts to turn, she won't get a mouthful of water or turn completely over.

5. Continue to pull her around the pool, or stay stationary if you are in a hot tub, for short periods of time. This will get her used to being on her own eventually.

# STEP SEVEN: "TURNING AND PULLING"

In this step, we start the baby out with dipping as always and then turn her over and start the pulling in the same motion. This step gets the baby ready for total independence in the water.

She will feel the water around her body and pretty soon you will find she doesn't need your hands supporting her any longer. She will be floating. Eventually the baby will get to the point where you can just start tapping one or two fingers underneath her head for support and she will be floating on her own.

# LEARNING TO "TURN AND PULL"

1. Count to three.

2. Blow in baby's face.

3. Skim the face through the water.

4. Lift the baby, turn, and start pulling in one motion.

**I can do it myself**

# STEP EIGHT: "INTO THE WATER FROM THE SIDE"

In this step, start by holding the child as he sits on the side of the pool. Then bring him forward into the water in one gentle motion. Help him come up and turn over so he starts feeling what it's like to go in from a height. Don't push the baby in. Gently ease him in at first. Just let him fall forward as if he were falling from the edge on his own. If you don't hesitate on this movement, he won't have a chance to inhale and take in water.

Sooner or later, the baby is bound to take a breath under the water. If he does get a mouthful, don't panic. Wait for his reaction before you react. He will usually spit it out, swallow it, or choke on it. If he comes up crying, bring him to your chest and comfort him. Take a quick rest and start again. Never stop the lesson on a negative note.

# STEP NINE: "HAVING FUN"

Continue practicing all your steps, but add "fun things" too.

**Wow, Mommy!**

## I. Take it slowly and gently.

We all know that children are brilliant. Their minds are like little sponges (they soak up everything), and if you take it slowly and gently, the child is going to progress faster than you ever thought possible. If you have a strong willed youngster, spend more time with him. Before you know it, he will be out-swimming all the rest of the children.

## 2. Start toddlers on their tummies.

Of course, toddlers must go through all the same swimming steps as the infants. Most of them, however, are not calm enough at first to start floating on their backs. So don't waste time pushing that step. They all want to "get up and go," so start them on their tummies first.

## 3. Kicking is most important!

Kicking is the main part of the child's stroke, so you must get the legs working first. If your child won't kick, put him on your shoulder and demonstrate with your hands rotating his calves. When he feels the movement, he will usually begin to kick. Once they get the kicking motion and feel the resistance of the water, most children will begin to do it on their own.

## 4. Tips on "Dipping" Toddlers, two, and three-year-olds.

If the child hasn't been in the water before two or three years old, he will be nervous and scared of both falling and going under the water. He won't want his face wet, so he will take a bit longer to acclimate. A baby usually loves the water, and you can start "dipping" the first day. You may have to surprise the two and three-year-olds, by going under with them the first few times. Whatever the circumstances, take your time and your efforts will be rewarded by not only having the best little swimmer, . . . but also the happiest.

## 5. Fins are important tools.

Swim fins help strengthen the legs, and give the child a feeling of confidence in his abilities. Since the fins are heavy on the child's legs, when he kicks, it begins to build up his leg muscles. They give him confidence because it enables him to get from one place to another easily and quickly. Fins can be used at almost any age, and they are wonderful tools for kicking.

## 6. "Floaties" can help the child learn to "get a breath."

    When the child begins to swim back and forth between the parents, or the parent and helper, you can use floaties to help him start coming up for a breath. Let him swim to you and if he doesn't lift his head up on his own, tap on his head to give him a reminder. Hold his chin and let him get a breath before he puts his head back down again. A few lessons working with the "floaties" will enable the child to start taking a breath without any help.

    You can also use the floaties with a child that is fearful. Just put them on and let the little one get used to being buoyant. Once they feel the floaties holding them up, they will want to swim on their own. After the child has become confident, you can start deleting the air in the floaties, gradually letting them deflate until the child is swimming by himself.

# 7. Taking off the flipper fins.

As soon as the child begins coming up for a breath, start taking the flipper fins off, one at a time. Let the child do a lesson with one flipper on the left foot and the next lesson on the right foot so as to strengthen both legs evenly. This may take a few lessons to accomplish so work with your child until he reaches that point. As soon as he is swimming on his own, you can practice with and without them on. He should be comfortable in both instances within a fairly short time.

## 8. Form is not important at this stage.

Your little one is not going to be swimming horizontally at first, lifting her head up for a breath and going back under again. She is going to lift up her head and hover for a moment as she takes a breath. You may even have to give her a gentle push on the back of the head to get her head back in a swimming position. Her body is tiny, and if she doesn't put her head back down quickly, she will stay in a vertical position. This "hovering" will stop eventually so don't be concerned by it. Just keep practicing.

## 9. They love "racing" dives!

Toddlers and older children love standing on the side of the pool to do "racing dives." Place the child's toes or flippers over the edge of the pool side. Bend her over with her hands down and in between her feet to support herself and help her balance. Then let her dive out to you. This may not be perfect at first so keep trying. Diving through a big hula hoop is helpful in getting the child to dive out instead of up.

## 10. Remember: Different Strokes for Different Folks.

A three-year-old naturally can stay under the water longer than a one-year-old. Eventually the one-year-old will get to where she can hold her breath as long as the three-year-old, but not at first. Different children will progress at different levels and at different times. There is no right or wrong time to begin.

## 11. Treat Time is important!

Your toddler or little one will love jumping off the side of the pool. As soon as he decides he is able to keep his head under the water, you can also teach him to dive for rings. You will be amazed to see how easy it is for your tiny one to go down three feet to the bottom and pick up a ring with a little help from you. Water logs (Styrofoam) can also be used for play and learning since they are not slippery, and the older children love inflatable crayons to ride on. Make sure you let your child do "fun" things right before playtime as a "treat."

**12. Always plan for twenty minutes of "play time" before taking the child out of the water after a lesson.**

It is very important to give the child a time of relaxation and play after the class. This will cement relations and promote wanting to come back and do this all over again.

# LESSONS FOR THE OLDER CHILD

With an older child, stick with one teacher. Go through all the steps that have been listed for the younger children, but with consideration for the fact that the child will probably be frightened if he has not learned to swim before four or older.

If the child is scared, start him out with fins and floaties to build up his confidence. This will start to develop trust in the instructor and enable him to advance more rapidly.

# PART THREE

# COME ON IN!

# THE WATER'S FINE

What a life — just me and my water log.

Are there any more rings for me to pick-up?

I'm tired!

I love you, Mommy!

49

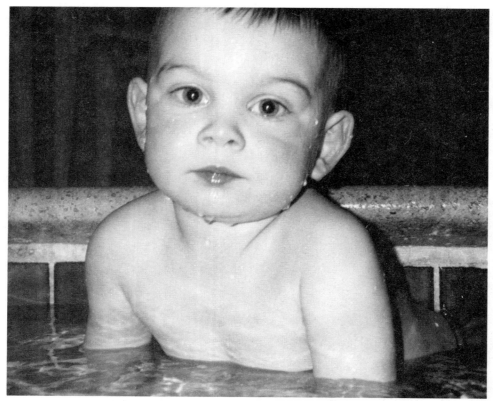

I'm not going to get out yet and you can't make me!

I can't believe I'm really going to swim.

**This is better than the beach.**

**I think this might be fun.**

Let go, Daddy — I'm ready to swim!

Hi, don't you just love my yellow goggles?

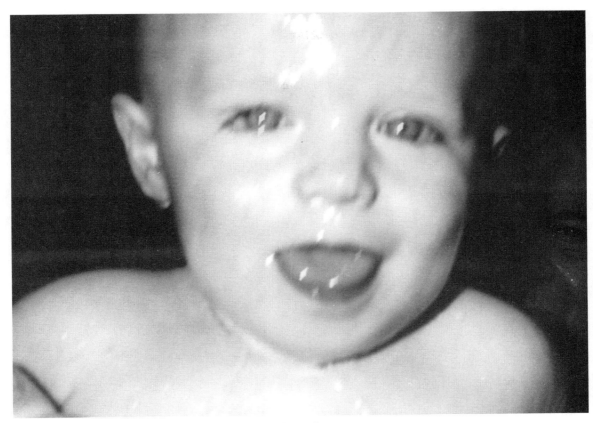

**All Smiles!**

53

**Real water babies!**

**Having fun with Mommy.**

This is the most fun I've ever had!

It's my ring, so don't get any ideas.

We're dry — but not for long.

And you thought I was standing on the bottom.

I love swimming with my sister.

Are you sure this is going to be fun?

I'm down here looking for starfish!

Mommy thinks I'm too, too wonderful for words.

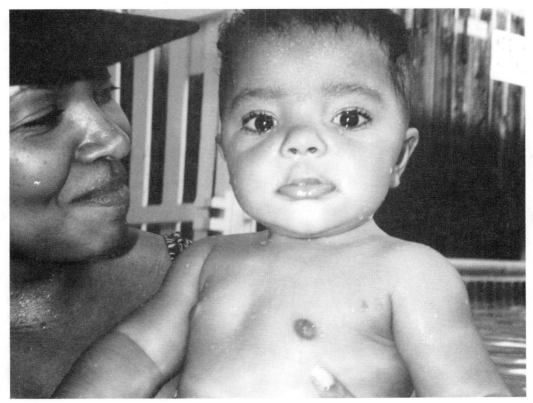

**Mommy is so proud of me.**

**Can we go up just a little higher?**

61

**I'd like to do this every day.**

**I can see under water with these!**

Let's get acquainted!

Stop talking and let's go!

63

**I'm only doing this for you, Mom!**

**Are you sure the water is 92°?**

**Are we getting out for lunch any time soon?**

**I just love swimming with my Dad!**

65

Isn't my new suit beautiful?

I guess I should have worn my visor.

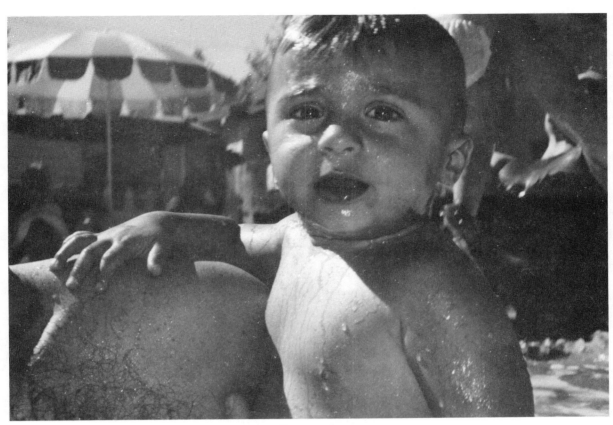

**Time for our lesson!**

**Family fun.**

**Diving and floating — what fun!**

**We love our rings.**

**Look at me, Daddy — I'm going under again!**

**I'm doing my big arms.**

**Trust
Between**

**Mom**

**and
Baby**

**Quality time with baby.**

**Having fun in my floaties.**

**I'm a little fish.**

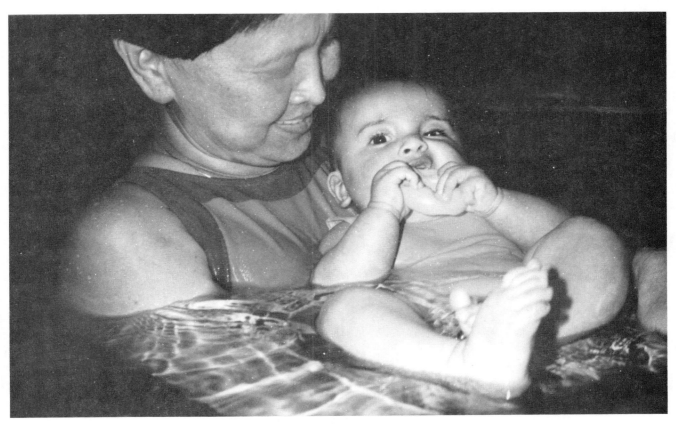

**Isn't this fun, Mommy?**

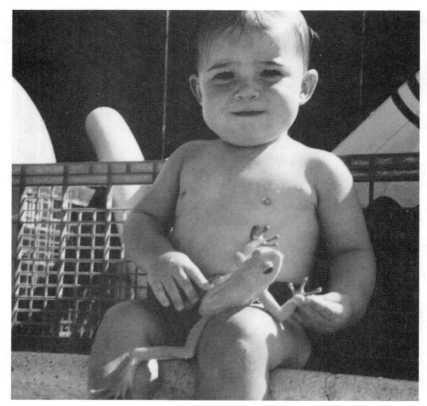

**I love my green frog.**

**Higher, Mommy! Higher!**

You can't catch me!

Here we are, all ready to swim.

Look everyone! Me and my toys are under water.

It's so much fun swimming with Mommy.

It's not time to get out, is it?

Ok, that's 3 laps. Now how many more should I do?

**Daddy and his girls.**

**I'm kicking as fast as I can.**

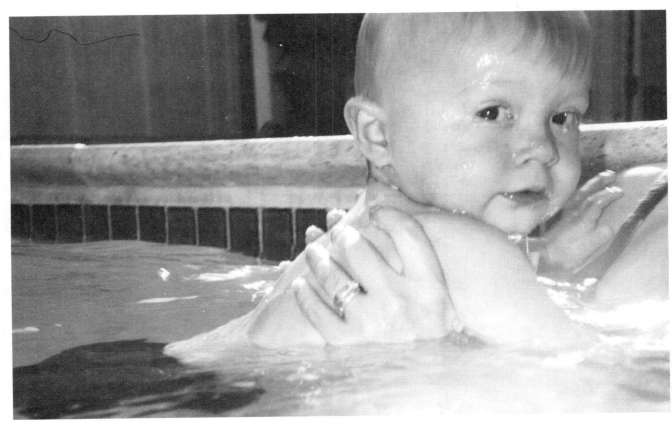

**Cute, aren't I?**

**Isn't this great swimming, Mom?**

**1 — 2 — 3 — Go!**

83

Everyone
needs a
hug
now
and
then

**I really love swimming!**

**Do I have to get out now?**

85

# CONCLUSION

Today Water Babies Swim School grows along with the children. Some of the original "water babies" are bringing their babies for lessons. The instructors work hard and are serious about their responsibilities, and in turn receive the satisfaction of smiling faces, gleeful hugs, "thank you"s from small lips, and the fulfillment of seeing children learning to love the water. But most rewarding to Gretchen, Gina, and the rest of the staff is knowing that they may have been instrumental in saving children's lives throughout the years.

Remember that no one, adult or child, is ever completely watersafe. A ten-year-old child can fall in the water and hit his head on the side and though he may be a good swimmer, he is not going to be able to save himself. Through these lessons, you are giving your baby more than a lifetime of fun and exercise. You are giving him or her a fighting chance in case of an accident. With as many pools and bodies of waters that there are in all areas of our country, there is no reason why a baby shouldn't learn to swim.

Accidental drownings of children happen every single summer with people who don't have covers on their pool or who turn their back for a moment. Swim lessons alone will not save a child's life. There must be constant supervision when around a pool. The pool needs to be covered and fenced in, and the parent or another responsible adult needs to be with the child at all times.

Our main purpose at Water Babies is to teach children to swim and to have a genuine respect for the water. It is our wish that after reading this book, you will come away with a greater knowledge for teaching your own children to be more comfortable and happy in the water.

Swimmingly,
Gina and Gretchen

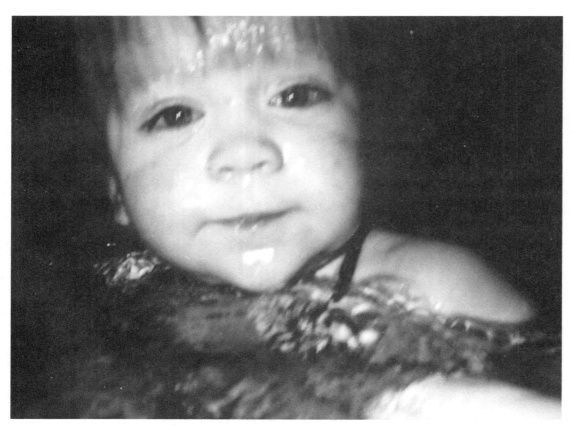

**I loved it and I'm coming back tomorrow!**

90

**Come back soon!**